SCARS
&
STRIPES

Fran Landesman

Golden Handshake

First published in 1997 by
Golden Handshake
8 Duncan Terrace
London N1 8BZ

With thanks to Jay, Simon, Nicki,
Howard, Tim and Jane

ISBN 0 905150 40 6

Designed and produced by Jane Havell
Cover design by Tony Cobb
Printed and bound by The Book Factory, London

Scars

Don't be ashamed
Everybody's got scars
From our various wars
On the way to the stars

Don't try to hide
Everybody's got scars
From crash landing on Mars
With these egos of ours

There's the one on your knee
Where you fell off your bike
Or the bite from a babe
That you love but don't like

There's the mess that you made
Without counting the cost
Or the cut from a blade
Or the child that you lost

Don't be ashamed
If you're covered with scars
On this planet of ours
That's the way we keep scores

So I'll show you my scars
If you show me yours
In the streets and the bars
Everybody's got scars
On their way to the stars
Everybody gets scars

FRAN LANDESMAN, born in Manhattan on 21 October 1927, has lived in London for over 33 years. She and her husband Jay Landesman wrote the book and lyrics for *The Nervous Set*, a musical satire on the Beat Generation which opened on Broadway in 1959, starring Larry Hagman as Jack Kerouac and Del Close as Allen Ginsberg. The score by Tommy Wolf included *Spring Can Really Hang You Up The Most* and *The Ballad of the Sad Young Men*, two numbers which have entered the popular musical canon. Regarded by the musical cognoscenti as the singer's songwriter, Fran's lyrics have provided material for Barbra Streisand, Ella Fitzgerald, Mabel Mercer, Bette Midler, Tony Bennett, Shirley Bassey, Rickie Lee Jones and Chaka Khan, whose records of her songs have sold millions.

Stage productions of her work include *Loose Connections, Invade My Privacy, Confessions of a Middle-Aged Juvenile Delinquent* and, on off-Broadway, *The Decline of the (Middle) West*. A Royal Shakespeare Company presentation of Joanna Hole's production of *There's Something Irresistible in Down* took place at The Young Vic in 1996.

Fran Landesman is a frequent broadcaster on BBC radio, and has performed on *Loose Ends, Kaleidoscope* and *Woman's Hour*, as well as making a guest appearance on *Desert Island Discs*.

Published collections of Fran Landesman's work include:
The Ballad of the Sad Young Men and Other Verse,
Polytantric Press, 1975
Invade My Privacy, Jonathan Cape, 1978
More Truth Than Poetry, The Permanent Press, 1979
Is It Overcrowded in Heaven?, Golden Handshake, 1981
The Thorny Side of Love, sun tavern fields, 1992
Rhymes at Midnight, Golden Handshake, 1996

Contents

Art

Me Again

Unlikely Wonders

Good Guys and Bad Guys

Scars

Art

Art

Art is anything that you can get away with
As someone I can't remember said
Art is any bright idea you want to play with
You don't need clever hands, it's in your head
You can work in skin, the living and the dead
A jar of piss, a drop of spit
A pile of bricks, a sack of shit
Encased in glass a pickled sheep
And can we laugh?
Or must we weep?

The Stolen Scream

They climbed a ladder and smashed a window
And stole The Scream
What fever possessed them to risk their freedom
To steal a dream?
Why bother?
The image is out there
Multiplied by millions
But not so surreal as a couple of thieves
Coming down a ladder
Carrying The Scream

Toilet Epigraphs

I've nothing to say
On toilet walls
But I do like to read
What the other girls
Have written in anger
Or written in smoke
To vent their frustration
Or just for a joke
A clean wall dismays me
"Write something," I plead
"I can't take a piss
Without something to read!"

Jeff Buckly

The boy had no time to grieve for
The father he'd never met
He knew too much to be happy
Too little to feel regret

He knew too much to be lucky
His short life was too intense
He gave it all to the music
The rest didn't make much sense

He slipped into the Mississippi River
Its muddy waters carried him away
The only thing that we can do is wonder
About the songs we'll never hear him play

He knew too much to be happy
But not too much to be great
The music lovers will miss him
Perhaps love came too late
Too bad he couldn't wait

Change

The unforgiving ethic of innovation
Has kept designers chasing after change
There isn't any future creating classics
When everybody wants a little strange

No matter how endearing your lifetime partner
The grass looks greener on another range
'Cause what's the fun of kissing the same old sweetie
When your libido needs a little strange

Visions of the new grow nastier
As the art on view gets ghastlier
    And emptier

As long as we continue in this direction
Sweet harmony grows harder to arrange
The unforgiving ethic of innovation
Has soured all our laughter
And kept us running after
The ever-dwindling promise
    Of change

Snapshots

Photographs are smiles that last forever
Snowmen that can never melt away
Birthday celebrations caught in amber
Rescued from the vaults of yesterday

Faces that were once more dear than diamonds
Boys who kept you up until the dawn
Houses filled with bicycles and babies
Ghosts who left their shadows on the lawn

Then turn the page
And see the children grow
The adults age
The lovers come and go

Photographs are holes in time's grey curtain
Through them we can peek into the past
Call upon our parents and our children
Pop a cork with members of the cast

There they are, the days of jazz and joy-rides
Snaps of magic moments lit by laughs
If you ever find my house on fire
        Leave the silver
        Save the photographs

The Lensman

His lens preserves the satin thigh
The pattern of the butterfly
He shows you faces that you know
The city, purified by snow
A battered banner in the breeze
The children of celebrities
The shadows of satanic mills
The flesh of unknown Jacks and Jills
The worm beneath the ivied wall
His flashing lens reveals it all
Concealing him behind its stare
He can't unbend. He'll never share
A moment when he looks absurd
      He fears the laugh
      And shuns the word

Pretty people waving from the balconies
Scent of spicy chicken on the summer breeze
Listen to the overlappin' harmonies
At the carnival

Multi-coloured mamas shake their massive curves
Dishin' up a smile with every dish they serves
Even the policemen don't get on their nerves
At the carnival

Now isn't it grand and isn't it great
The sound of the band is telling you, mate
There's fun to be found
Start lookin' around
It isn't too late

Everybody's rockin' to the steady beat
Flowing like a river rolling down the street
Always on the lookout for a friend to greet
At the carnival

Everybody's waving as the floats go by
Happy as a humming-bird and twice as high
Who's that little beauty giving you the eye?
Oh me, oh my
What a carnival!

Music

Music reaches places
That nothing else can reach
Brings back scenes and faces
More vividly than speech

Music conjures memories
Of summers at the beach
Songs recall emotions
More vividly than speech

Isn't it strange how potent old tunes can be
Bits of your life get hooked on a melody
Music can lift your spirits or break your heart
Open your soul with the delicate blade of art

Music starts us weeping
When no one is around
Music fills the darkness
With visions made of sound

Music travels with us
A witness and a crutch
Music reaches places
That nothing else can touch

Close Call

Your bet, tough shot
Close call, tight spot
Big race, you're in the lead
Fast cars, dangerous speed

So far, so good
Close call, touch wood
You can fold if you choose
Next time maybe you'll lose

Taking chances for the thrill of your life
Doing dances on the edge of a knife
Watching others going into a spin
Flying brothers who are dying to win

Close call, hard case
He's played his ace
Next time maybe you'll fall
This time
It's a real close call

Metamorphosis

Friends keep turning into strangers
All our bubbles glow then pop
Maybe it's the stuff we're taking
But we just don't want to stop

Guys who used to be so funny
Sit and watch the tulips grow
Everybody's getting stranger
Though it doesn't always show

They get busy feeding pigeons
They get dizzy breeding wealth
They get hung on new religions
Or the hot pursuit of health

Jill who used to look so pretty
Sticks her pay cheque up her nose
Beauty doesn't seem to matter
That's the way this garden grows

On my way to somewhere crucial
I forget the debts I owe
Friends keep turning into strangers
Bread keeps turning into snow

Me Again

Old-Fashioned Girl

If you want me to cut a thinner slice
You must get me a sharper knife
If you want me to sing another song
You must give me another life
If you want me to smile a different smile
You must tell me a different tale
For I am a girl who was raised to trust
In the wisdom of the male

I'll Be Seeing Me

I'll be seeing me
With all my old familiar faces
All my fetching airs and graces
Through the years
In a summer dress
A damsel in distress
A Greenwich Village vamp
A little coy, a little camp

I'll be seeing me
In every lovely colour spread
Reclining on my famous bed
Recalling all the lives I've led
I'll see me in the looking glass
And when you bring the tea
I'll be looking at your ass
But I'll be seeing me

Either it's rule or be ruled
Either it's fool or be fooled
Either it's jump or get jumped on
Either it's dump or get dumped on
Either way – there's a price to pay

Either it's catch or get caught
Etiher it's buy or be bought
Either it's smart or it's boring
Either it's art or it's whoring
Either way – you'll get old some day

It's a mean old scene
And the competition's vicious
If your hands are clean
You're the one who's done the dishes

Either it's sharp or it's flat
Either it's dog or it's cat
Either it's beat or get beaten
Either it's eat or get eaten
If you go, or decide to stay
Either way – there's a price to pay

I Don't Know

Why can't people say "I don't know"?
What self-confidence it would show
When asked where? how? or why?
To reasonably reply – "I don't know . . .
Haven't a clue . . . Not the foggiest . . .
Can't help you . . . Awfully sorry . . .
I don't know"
Instead they keep you waiting at intersections
While they search their mental attics
For the wrong directions
They keep you dangling while they pretend
They'll come up with the answer in the end
If you'll just hold your hat and hang on half a mo' –
Do they think it would come as a terrible blow
If they let a small gap in their expertise show?
I don't know.

The Kindness of Strangers

I've always relied on the kindness of strangers
To lift up my spirits and meet me halfway
I hope that we're in for a marvellous evening
There aren't many rules that we have to obey

My passion is people, the stranger the better
At least they won't bore you with maudlin clichés
I've always relied on the kindness of strangers
As someone remarked in dear Tennessee's play

This world can be a lonely place
It's hard to win the human race
But if you're willing to risk some pain
One day you'll run into fun again

There's no way of knowing just where we are going
Or what may be waiting around the next bend
But in all your travels the moments to treasure
Are those when a stranger turns into a friend

When you've tried and you've tried
And there's no place to hide
And you can't cadge a ride
With no God on your side
I have always relied
On the kindness of strangers

The Compulsive Talker

Don't think that I don't adore you
When I try to speed you on your way
But I'm a compulsive talker
And I can't abide the things I say

At parties I'm best avoided
When somebody asks me how I feel
I don't spare the gruesome details
As I see their friendly smiles congeal

And once again I'm saying
Things I've said before
About a jazz revival or a nuclear war
And I feel my face go crimson
With embarrassment
And I haven't said a single thing
I've really meant

I once was a party person
Now it's time for me to fade away
Or else I'll go right on talking
And I really hate the things I say

Epiphany on the A-Train

The train shoots out of the dark
And on to the bridge
In a dazzle of daylight the billboard sings
"Believe in Christ the Lord and thou shalt be saved"
Why do the words thrill
My unbelieving teenage soul?
The message I receive
Has little to do with a crucified Jew
And everything to do with the sound of the words
Marvellous in my mouth
"We are poetry," they sing to me
"And poetry is the way and the life"

The products of my talent
Give such a paltry light
My rhymes are little glow-worms
That decorate the night
Their ineffectual fire
Cannot illuminate
The mysteries of desire
The puzzles of our state

An Educated Guess

It seems to me you're flirting with disaster
You're gonna wind up in a mess
I don't have any inside information
That's just an educated guess

You really look sensational this evening
I'm feeling things I can't express
But I'm prepared to hear you say it's over
That's just an educated guess

I don't claim to be clairvoyant
After all I could be wrong
But I've been around a little
And I've heard a lot of songs
Nothing magic lasts for long

I'll probably find someone else to play with
Another beauty in distress
I'll be her friend while trying to forget you
That's just an educated guess

Perhaps when you grow tired of the high life
You may discover more is less
And then you'll see that we belong together
That's just an educated guess
Merely an educated guess

Who Needs People?

I hear people
Talking about "their people"
I don't have any people
I've never had any people
I've had friends and lovers
Collaborators and playmates
But I don't call them "my people"
I've got sons and a grandson and a brother
But I don't say – "have your people call my people"
Where are my people?
Do I want any people?
No. I'm not a person who needs people –
I'd rather have friends

Baby Daze

You're growing up, baby mine
You've recognised your reflection
I saw you give it a kiss
Yes, it's adorable
But somewhere ahead
Some one of your sunny, summer days
The time will come
To introduce you
To your shadow

A Libran Dilemma

To begin with I despised astrology
As the last refuge of ageing chorus girls
Friends of Mother's who rattled along in a varicose vein
While I flirted with Marxist dream boys
I travelled with the radicals
Because I loved their songs
But the icy voice of reason whispered treason to the cause
That was long ago
When we all believed in butter
And no one suspected that sunshine could give you cancer

Now that everyone is polarised
We wishy-washy liberals are the more despised
The ones who believe are so angry and so pure
While the ones who know it isn't so
Are so scornful and so sure
I've begun to blame my star sign
For my double vision, my awful indecision
Still longing to belong

Socialism looked good on paper
It was only people who needed perfecting
I still prefer the poetry of revolution
To mean, monetarist theology
But either way there's a price to pay
As black and white melt into grey

To begin with I despised astrology
Now I read about it with amused condescension
And part of my apology for dithering
Includes the fact that I was born
Under the blind, scale-carrying star

A Moaner's Boast

My favourite pastime is moaning
'Cause moaning is what I do best
I try to be bitter but witty
While getting the blues off my chest

My hero is dear Victor Meldrew
The Mozart of kvetch and complaint
The Disney of dissatisfaction
I claim him for my patron saint

I see my bridges flaming
And mourn my shattered dream
But I'll succeed in claiming
A place on the British whingeing team

When fate makes me stagger or stumble
I hope that I grumble with style
I do it the better for knowing
That things will get worse in a while

Is Anyone There?

Does something look into our minds
And study our intentions?
Does something see our secret souls
Not just our sweet inventions?

Does something judge our random moves
As though we really mattered?
Does something understand the way
That love can leave us shattered?

If there is a life hereafter
I wonder where I'll dwell
I'm not good enough for heaven
Not bad enough for hell

Does something watch our every twitch
And catch the sparrow straying?
Does something look into our hearts
And hear us when we're praying?

Does something cause the sun to rise,
And give your mother cancer?
I only pose these questions, folks,
I do not have the answer

It Comes and It Goes

I've seen meaning melt away
And I've seen stars reborn
I've seen artists make it big
Then burn to dust in rage and scorn

That's life I suppose. It comes and it goes
You miss by a mile or win by a nose
Whatever you choose – it comes and it goes

Sometimes nothing moves at all
For what may seem like years
Then there comes a sudden storm
That leaves you joy or floods of tears

That's life I suppose. It comes and it goes
So shoot for the moon or stay home and dose
Whatever you do – it comes and it goes

I've seen love in someone's eyes
And I've seen eyes grow cold
I've seen babies learn to walk
And bits of beauties growing old

That's life I suppose. It comes and it goes
A door opens wide. Another will close
You miss by a mile or win by a nose
Whatever you do – it comes and it goes

A Better Way

On every side the killers ride
The bloody road to fame
From Crosmer Glen to Bethlehem
The bullets sound the same

They know they're right. Their eyes burn bright
With pride in what they've done
And when they fall God save them all
For each was someone's son

Chorus:
There's gotta be a better way
The death toll's mounting day by day
They're killing for the cause they say
But there's gotta be a better way

If you and I, my honey pie
Do battle every day
What hope is there the world can share
To find a better way

What can we do, Muslim and Jew
Protestant or I.R.A.
One won't concede, the others need
So terror rules! O.K.?

There's gotta be a better way
A better game for men to play
'Cause Jesus Christ was born they say
To show us all a better way

From Bethlehem to Crosmer Glen
There's a bloody price to pay
On Christmas morn a child was born
To show the world a better way
      Or so they say

The Void

Watching dead friends on the telly
Served by a rusty old droid
What have I found to replace you
Only the usual void

Travelling far from my home world
Feeling a bit paranoid
What do I see from the porthole
Only the usual void

We've been hammered by different gravities
On the anvils of worlds far apart
We've been diving for treasure in different seas
But I've saved you a place in my heart

Maybe some day we'll discover
Gods that we thought we'd destroyed
Everything else disappearing
Into the usual void

This Life

This life is fickle and fragmented
Some shows will run and run
Sometimes the deal that you've cemented
Gets foiled and spoils your fun

Some say this life is overrated
Too bad we can't live twice
The virgins say "be glad you waited"
The punters roll the dice

Perhaps it's just an episode
In a drama that continues
And life is just another road
That leads to other venues

This life is fabulous and funny
So let's not fuss and fret
Or waste it chasing after money
Or soil it with regret
It may be all we get

So fragile are the women and the men
        After this life
How can we live again?

Overture (to corrupt and deprave)

I was put on this planet
To corrupt and deprave you
So prepare for your ruin
'Cause nothing can save you

I've been planning your futures
I hope you'll enjoy them
If you have any morals
I plan to destroy them

We'll nibble on each others lips
And share a special bottle of wine
I'll listen to your fantasies
And guide you through the jungle of mine

I will give you a dream life
Full of poison and pleasure
And some bittersweet memories
I hope you will treasure

I will show you a landscape
Of desire and danger
When the loving is over
I'll still be a stranger

The War

"The biggest haul we've ever made"
The coppers proudly boast
"We caught the smugglers bang to rights
We stopped them at the coast"

But there isn't a shortage. The price isn't rising
With all of the drug busts that's rather surprising
It reaches consumers without advertising
They're losing the war against drugs

God gave us these flowers, they soothe and inspire
They grow just like weeds and there's always a buyer
'Cause people just naturally want to get higher
Seems humans can't do without drugs

Dig back in the history of nations and races
The students and diggers come up with the traces
Of substances used to put smiles on the faces
Of Romans and Druids, in smoke or in fluids

In pipes and bowls and jugs
Humanity always did drugs
In spite of finks and bugs
They're losing the war against drugs

In the Name of Love

He could have been a dustman or a cabbie
He could have been an ordinary cove
It really was too bad he was a bishop
But what he did was in the name of love

In the name of love
He had no strategy
In the name of love
He courted tragedy

But were those stolen kisses really evil
Offending God in heaven up above?
They say that he was tempted by the devil
But what he did was in the name of love

In the name of love
In the name of love
Oh how he suffered
In the name of love

Unlikely Wonders

Have I wasted my time waiting for unlikely wonders
Have I wasted my life waiting for a phone to ring
Will my projects and plans stumble on their own
         pretensions
Will I ever succeed like the cherry trees this spring?

Waiting for unlikely wonders
Praying that my paper planes will fly
Filling up the empty hours
Smoking dope and trying not to cry

Waiting for the magic moment
Rooting for another hopeless cause
Yesterday it looked so easy
Now it seems they've put my dreams on pause

I search the heavens
There goes another star
Unlikely wonders
I wonder where you are

Time and time again I ponder
Signs and omens somewhere in the sky
Waiting for unlikely wonders
Tell me they may happen by and by
Say I'm gonna fly
Bye and bye

Annabel Dominatrix

No daffodil blooms out of turn in her garden
No clumsy young man is permitted a slip
No animal roars out of turn in her circus
They all love to dance to the crack of her whip

With ultimate scorn she dismisses a suitor
Her heart has been mangled and locked in a chest
The beautiful Annabel booted and belted
Is really a prisoner just like all the rest

They stand in line to catch a glimpse
Of her resplendent hips
But never hear the weary sigh
Escaping from her lips

The beautiful Annabel strokes her Alsatian
As nightly the ritual violence unfurls
She plays the tormentress relentless in leather
But hiding inside is the sad little girl

Who Can You Trust? (shallow grave)

If you can't trust your friends
Who can you trust?
If you haven't got pals
Life is a bust
You're a broken machine
Starting to rust
If you can't trust your friends
Who can you trust?

If you can't trust your mates
What can you do?
There's a corpse in the bed
Waiting for you
You can say it's a dream
But what if it's true?
If you can't trust your friends
What can you do?

When you've got friends to share the cave
You laugh with Alex, dance with Dave
You face your fear each time you shave
And try to forget about the shallow grave

If your friends let you down
Where do you go?
You're alone and in pain
Lost in the snow
So you hang on and hope
You've got them sussed
If you can't trust your friends
Who can you trust?

Chameleons

We've been out there before
Where the scene-makers move
Showing off our old tricks
On the lookout for love

In the dream before last
We were sure we would win
We could mirror their minds
We were bound to fit in

Chameleons know how to survive
We change our colours to suit the scene
Though times are strange, chameleons will thrive
We know the omens and what they mean

We were doing O.K.
Till they gave us the air
And we're gonna be fine
With a little repair

We'll pretend to be friends
As we were in the past
But we've altered a lot
Since the dream before last

Chameleons will always arrive
In changing colours and shifting shapes
Chameleons know how to survive
A mood may trap us but we'll escape
Just by changing our skin
We can always fit in

The King of Cool

The Queen of Love and Beauty and the King of Cool
Got married in St Louis by a swimming pool
Their wedding party ended in the swimming pool

The king had been a hero in the war-stained sky
But marriage made him jumpy as the years went by
Dope helped him to remember how it felt to fly

He had always been a gambler
Till it all became a drag
And the people that he ran with
Left the king to hold the bag
The people that he trusted
Stood by while he got busted

They say he kept a notebook with a list of names
The ones who bought his goodies and enjoyed his games
Rich citizens got caught up in his fun and games

The citizens all wonder what the courts will hear
The King of Cool is certain there's not much to fear
He's far too old and far too ill to feel much fear

And if you were one of his customers
Don't lose your sense of humour
Maybe that list he kept
Was just a rumour

Nicki's Dilemma

Damned if you do / damned if you don't
Damned if he will / damned if he won't
If he doesn't call / you wake up in hell
But if he falls . . . Oh well

Damned if you lose / damned if you win
Damned if you're straight / damned if you sin
Some days you can dance / and everything's swell
Till you recall . . . Oh well

Damned if you give him everything
Damned for holding back
I know a girl with everything
But she's under attack
When her blues turn to black

     She's –
Damned if she runs / damned if she stays
Damned if she flirts / damned if she prays
Now she's looking for / a guru or a guide
Looking for a door / or somewhere to hide

She longs to go back / and find the old buzz
But she's damned if she does

The Fucking You're Getting

From the moment you met him
The whole thing was upsetting
Is the fucking you're getting
Worth the fucking you're getting?

You should make a decision
There's no object in fretting
Is your current arrangement
Worth the fucking you're getting?

When the two of you are skin to skin
The sensation is delicious
When the screwing's through you just can't win
'Cause at heart he's really vicious

Though you love every moment
Of the kissing and petting
There's a cynical sister
Who will tell you she's betting
That you'll soon be regretting
All the fucking you're getting

The Piano Player

There's a shy piano player
Who is looking for a tune
That will move a music-lover
On a rainy afternoon

There's a shy piano player
Who is dreaming of a break
That will turn him into Gershwin
For his dear old mother's sake

He's a shy piano player
And he knows some pretty licks
Though he doesn't make much money
He can always pull the chicks

There's a singer in the spotlight
Who is taking lots of bows
Though she gives him all the credit
That his modesty allows

There's an undiscovered genius
Hid behind a baby grand
He's a shy piano player
Who deserves a great big hand
(And he's always in demand)

The Good Guys and the Bad

You can't tell the good guys from the bad guys
You can't tell the righteous from the rats
> We used to be so sure
> Our hearts were brave and pure
We took such pride in being democrats

Now we all sit on the fence
Buggered by ambivalence
No one knows what move to make
No one knows which side to take

You can't tell the good guys from the bad guys
You can't spot the spoilers any more
> The heroes of the left
> Are stained by greed and theft
The other lot are rotten to the core

Once we knew which side was right
Black was black and white was white
We're so well informed today
Everything's a shade of grey

Today everybody's got an angle
You can't tell a hero from a heel
> The country's going bust
> There's no one you can trust
When everybody's looking for a deal

And everybody triple locks their door
'Cause you can't tell the good guys
From the bad guys any more

From Pat's Letter

I buy liquor in tiny bottles
So I can have a drink after dinner
Without waking up
To finish the bottle in the morning
Which, of course, wrecks the day
Not to mention the life

After the Party (for Rosie Gibb)

Rosie in the shining water
Mother courage, Erin's daughter
Swmming topless in November
One dark day I will remember
Sequin sun and Rosie right on
Rising from the sea at Brighton

Men Who Love Mermaids

Men who love mermaids
Will never recover
Men who love mermaids
Are always at sea
Tangled in forests
Where mermaids keep lovers
Swaying in seaweeds
That won't set them free

Underneath the waves
In the spangled light of love
They cannot be reached
By a message from above

Men who love mermaids
Are made for surrender
Glad to be victims
Or passionate slaves
Men who love mermaids
Are lost in a blue world
Happy to linger
In watery graves

Video Kid

He's a video kid
Playing faster and faster
He plays video games
Just avoiding disaster

He makes baddies explode
At the push of a button
In his fantasy world
He's an ace, not a shut-in

No ball games, no blue skies
No acres of green
A small boy alone
With a video screen

He won't climb the big trees
Like his daddy once did
And he doesn't need friends
He's a video kid

Some Boys

Some boys can tell how you feel
From the look in your eyes
Some boys can read it in your face
Some boys don't care how you feel
They're just horny young guys
Some boys will put you in your place

Some will have you singing a song
    On easy street
Some just like to string you along
    And then retreat

Some boys will linger around
On the edge of your life
Some boys will touch your heart and run
Some boys will leave you to walk
On the edge of a knife
Some boys just want a little fun

Some boys will buy you pretty toys
Some boys just make a lot of noise
This girl admires and enjoys – some boys
Some boys use clever little ploys
Some boys have smiles that wreck your poise
This girl desires and enjoys – some boys

All the best heroes have feet of clay
Good guys and leaders get led astray
Makers of laws they cannot obey
Everyone's heroes have feet of clay

Rock-and-roll singers and feminists
Racers and boxers with deadly fists
Mother Teresa, Big Bird and O.J.
Everyone's heroes have feet of clay

Slogans and certainties can't be trusted
Princes have strayed and Popes have lusted
Healers and heroes can lose their grip
Aren't they entitled to one little slip?

Do we expect them to toe the line
True to their image and stiff of spine
Wearing the white hat and never the grey?
All the best heroes have feet of clay
We must discover the truth some day
When we read about those feet of clay

Are You Lookin' At Me?

Are you lookin' at me?
That's not too smart
I could sting like a bee
Or break your heart

Are you lookin' at me?
What's on your mind?
Do you like what you see?
Am I well designed?

I don't wanna bust your bubble
I hate to spoil your fun
But you're gonna get in trouble
If I were you I'd run

Are you lookin' at me?
You'd better not
Odds on gettin' home free
Are not so hot

If you're lookin' about
For a random thrill
Then you're gonna find out
That a look can kill

Scars

You're the Grounds in my Coffee

You're the grounds in my coffee
You're the stone in my shoe
You're the fly in my ointment
I could do without you

You're the worm in my apple
You're the cloud in my sky
You're the drunk at my party
I keep wondering why –

Why I think about you
Everywhere I go
Why the world without you
Seems a little slow

You're the flaw in my theory
You're the bill in my mail
You're the hammer that hits me
And just misses the nail

You're the reason I mutter
That I wish I was dead
You're the leak in my dreamboat
You're the hole in my head
You're the grounds in my coffee
You're the crumb in my bed

Love isn't included in our deal
So treat me like a brother
No show business hugs or friendly feels
'Cause one thing leads to another

I won't even try to touch your heart
With this, that or the other
'Cause after the fun we'll fall apart
As one thing leads to another

I won't be extending any invitations
Or trying to attract your eye
We don't want to start any tricky situations
That will lead to complications
By and by

Whatever I feel for you, old dear
I know I'd better smother
I may get a lift when you appear
But a lift can lead to a reckless deed
As one thing leads
To another
As one thing feeds
Into another

Down

Down has some terrible attractions
Featuring desperate distractions
And that hooker Misery
Sings "I'll never set you free"
'Cause there's something irresistible in down

Down makes some dangerous suggestions
Taunts you with sweet depressing questions
You can tell yourself to quit
But you really must admit
That there's something irresistible in down

When you're up down doesn't matter a damn
You keep thinking Wow! How lucky I am!
Then you trip or slip on Misery's scam
And you can't help falling
The grave is calling

It's swell to do a little slumming
You think that sad is so becoming
Till the room begins to spin
And the funnel sucks you in
And you wake up in the scary part of town
Finding something irresistible in down

You continue to enjoy yourself
While trying to destroy yourself
There's something irresistible in down

The Dream Before Last

In the dream before last
We were hot as a stove
Here we go once again
On the lookout for love

We've been out there before
Where the dream-makers move
Showing off our old tricks
On the lookout for love

The dream before last was insanely great
A fabulous future in view
I thought we were heading for heaven's gate
How sad that it didn't come true
I shouldn't be speaking to you

I was walking on air
Till you gave me a shove
Here we go once again
On the lookout for love

We pretend to be friends
As we were in the past
But we've grown up a lot
Since the dream before last

Now and Then

We all get evil thoughts, now and then
We all get lost or caught, yet again
We all get tense and terrified
We all get taken for a ride
We all have thoughts of suicide
Every now and then

It's like the Twilight Zone, now and then
We hate to walk alone, after ten
The shameful dreams we never tried
Start festering like sores inside
The doors of hell fall open wide
Every now and then

I'll get a lucky break, who knows when?
I'm truly wide awake, now and then
And when my moment comes along
I'll make my move and sing my song
Before it all starts going wrong, yet again

I'll take the joy that comes along
Every now and then

Tell It On the Telly

Got a problem?
Don't let it defeat you
Dad abused you?
Your husband beat you?
Don't keep it to yourself
Or confide it to a friend
Just spill it on the telly
The modern way to mend

You've been cheated
Lied to and misguided?
Go on telly
Don't try to hide it
It's gonna cost you big
If you tell it to the shrinks
But spill the mess to Esther
And she'll celebrate your kinks

No matter how smelly your husband's feet
Tell all on the telly and they'll smell sweet
Just bring along your children
Your husband and your lover
And treat them to a day out
From which they won't recover

Tell your story
And don't be a victim
You took punches
Now you inflict 'em
Your mother put you down
And called you a giraffe?

Your daddy tied you up
And chopped your cat in half?
You can tell it on the telly
And give everyone a laugh

A Monster in the Making

Sitting in the park watching the babies
Is never boring
A small girl falls stoically again and again
She falls without a sound
No one seems to notice
Finally she starts to scream
Till it seems her lungs will burst
I ponder her future
Will she be an artist
Or do I see
A monster in the making?

Mugged by a Memory

Mugged by a memory
In broad daylight
Stabbed by what used to be
But wasn't quite . . .

Mugged by a memory
Under blue sky
The ghost of you and me
In days gone by

I crumple up the lethal image
And chuck it in my mental bin
I drag myself back to the present
Where the blues begin

Mugged by a memory
Pulled by the past
Fooled by a comedy
That didn't last

Mornings we'd lie in bed
The world forgot
Nights we'd get high in bed
Happy or what?

I try to mend my mood with humour
And arm against the next attack
I tell myself I must be crazy
I wouldn't want you back

Trying to change the tune
Your face I see
On this bright afternoon
The past is stalking me
I've been mugged
By a memory

The Star

The star was in hell
The audience fell
In love with the shell
They never spied
The raw, sad, squirming
Thing inside
Till the shell fell
Into disrepair
And we caught the smell
Of a star's despair

The Pushers and the Pushed

The pushers and the pushed
The sussers, the sussed
The takers, the taken
And those who can't be shaken

The movers, the moved
The crimes that can't be proved
The liars, the lied to
The criers and the cried to

The spenders, the spent
The kids without a cent
The sleepers on cement
The straight, the bent

The makers, the made
Who make us feel afraid
The leaders, the led
The living, the dead

The breakers, the busted
The awfully well adjusted
When all is done and dusted –
Can anyone be trusted?

Time is the Beast

Time is the beast
Feasting on beauty's face
Biting the dancer's ankles
Trumping the hero's ace

Time is the beast
Grinding our dreams to dust
Wearing away our courage
Watering down our lust

See your pretty babies
Reaching out for more
Growing into strangers
Walking out the door
Time will steal the sparkle
From those baby eyes
Searching for an answer
Pleading for a prize

Time is the beast
Waiting to pull you down
Tearing the lost to tatters
Stealing the winner's crown

Time wears away
Friends we can spare the least
What does it all add up to?
Just another feast
For the beast

The Whip of Words

Who is holding the whip of words
Inside your mind?
Who is holding the smoking torch
That makes you blind?

What old devil is whispering
Into your ear
Catalogues of your darkest deeds
The things you fear?

You used to live in sunshine
With strawberries and cream
And loving in the morning
To wake you from your dream

What's become of your chummy world?
The friends you had?
Who has turned you against yourself
And made you mad?

Why did everything fall apart?
You must be dreaming
Once you lived with a happy heart
And now you're screaming

The Grand Illusion Bar

You will find the strangest fishes
Swimming nightly in this jar
Everybody's got a story
In the Grand Illusion Bar

Though the easy money vanished
With your flashy suit and car
It is still the roaring Eighties
In the Grand Illusion Bar

If you can't take the funky language
Stick your fingers in your ears
'Cause the punters get pretty basic
They'll reduce a fool to tears
It's not a bit like Cheers!

Better save your true confessions
They won't get you very far
Fantasy is what's on offer
In the Grand Illusion Bar

You may bump into a villain
Or a fading movie star
No one cares how big you are
You can share a little glory
Everybody's got a story
In the Grand Illusion Bar

Waiter, the Check!

It used to be a great life
But now it's just a wreck
I think it's time to pack it in
Waiter, the check!

The starters were delicious
I binged, but what the heck
Now I admit I'm sick of it
Waiter, the check!

Sometimes it was rewarding
Some fame and other stuff
I can't complain that I loved in vain
But enough, is enough, is enough

I hate to think I'm only
A pain in someone's neck
I've had my fill. Let's have the bill
Waiter, please bring the check!